ALTERNATOR
BOOKS™

SOCCER SUPER STATS

JEFF SAVAGE

Lerner Publications ◆ Minneapolis

Lerner Publications Company
A division of Lerner Publishing Group, Inc.
241 First Avenue North
Minneapolis, MN 55401 USA

For reading levels and more information, look up this title at www.lernerbooks.com.

Main body text set in Aptifer Sans LT Pro 12/18.
Typeface provided by Linotype AG.

Library of Congress Cataloging-in-Publication Data

Title: Soccer super stats / Jeff Savage.
Description: Minneapolis : Lerner Publications, [2018] | Series: Pro sports stats | Includes bibliographical references and index.
Identifiers: LCCN 2016058432 (print) | LCCN 2016059913 (ebook) | ISBN 9781512434095 (lb : alk. paper) | ISBN 9781512449488 (eb pdf)
Subjects: LCSH: Soccer—Records—Juvenile literature.
Classification: LCC GV943.25 .S29 2018 (print) | LCC GV943.25 (ebook) | DDC 796.334—dc23

LC record available at https://lccn.loc.gov/2016058432

Manufactured in the United States of America
1-42045-23915-3/3/2017

TABLE OF CONTENTS

SPANNING THE GLOBE

n 1930 Uruguay hosted soccer's first-ever World Cup. About 60,000 fans attended the championship match, won by Uruguay. In 1950 Uruguay won the World Cup crown again. That tournament's final match in Brazil drew 199,854 fans! By then soccer had become the most popular sport in the world. The game on the field hasn't changed much since its early days. What has changed are the statistics, or stats, available to fans.

What are soccer's greatest and most revealing statistics? First, you should know more about the biggest leagues and tournaments.

UNITED STATES AND CANADA

Major League Soccer (MLS) is the top professional league in the United States. Average attendance at soccer-only stadiums is higher than that of the National Basketball Association (NBA) and the National Hockey League (NHL). Youth soccer in North America is booming. Even in hockey-loving Canada, soccer is the most popular sport among children. As the sport's popularity grows, more and more fans will turn to stats to tell soccer's stories.

2016 COLORADO RAPIDS

WORLDWIDE

Soccer is called football everywhere except the United States and Canada. There are more than 3.5 billion soccer fans worldwide. The oldest soccer competition in the world is the Football Association Challenge Cup (FA Cup), played in England since 1872. Other European leagues host popular yearly contests that draw millions of fans.

The Fédération Internationale de Football Association (FIFA) governs soccer around the world. The FIFA World Cup is held in a different country every four years. The tournament is the top prize in international soccer. Soccer has been an official sport of the Olympic Games since 1900. Since the early 1990s, women have had their own World Cup and Olympic tournaments.

1930 WORLD CUP

CHAPTER ONE

PLAYER SUPER STATS

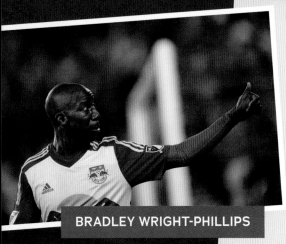

BRADLEY WRIGHT-PHILLIPS

THE GOLDEN BOOT

Scoring a goal is the dream of most young soccer athletes. The moment the ball enters the goal, you are a star. If the goal wins the game, you are a hero. It is one of the best feelings in sports. A player who scores a lot of goals must have skill—and a little luck. Since 2005 each season's leading scorer in MLS has received the Golden Boot award.

MLS Golden Boot Winners

SEASON	PLAYER	TEAM	GOALS
2016	Bradley Wright-Phillips	New York Red Bulls	24
2015	Sebastian Giovinco	Toronto FC	22
2014	Bradley Wright-Phillips	New York Red Bulls	27
2013	Camilo Sanvezzo	Vancouver Whitecaps FC	22
2012	Chris Wondolowski	San Jose Earthquakes	27
2011	Dwayne De Rosario	D.C. United	16
2010	Chris Wondolowski	San Jose Earthquakes	18
2009	Jeff Cunningham	FC Dallas	17
2008	Landon Donovan	LA Galaxy	20
2007	Luciano Emilio	D.C. United	20
2006	Jeff Cunningham	Real Salt Lake	16
2005	Taylor Twellman	New England Revolution	17

PREMIER EVENT

In 1863 the Football Association of England was formed. It was the sport's first organization to oversee rules and matches. Around then the residents of the English town of Sheffield invented rules such as **corner kicks** and **free kicks** that are still used around the world.

In modern England, the Premier League is the country's top soccer league. Alan Shearer, the Premier League's all-time leading goal scorer, was honored in 2016 with a statue that stands at St. James Park, where he played for Newcastle United.

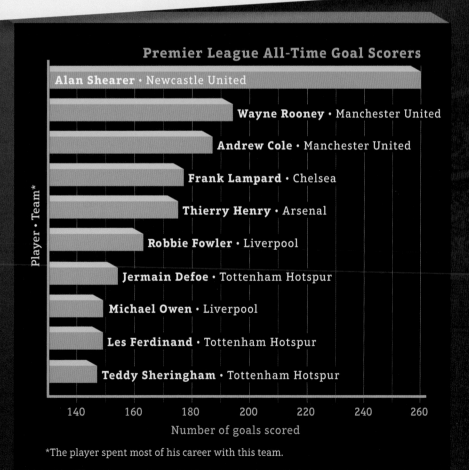

Premier League All-Time Goal Scorers

- **Alan Shearer** · Newcastle United
- **Wayne Rooney** · Manchester United
- **Andrew Cole** · Manchester United
- **Frank Lampard** · Chelsea
- **Thierry Henry** · Arsenal
- **Robbie Fowler** · Liverpool
- **Jermain Defoe** · Tottenham Hotspur
- **Michael Owen** · Liverpool
- **Les Ferdinand** · Tottenham Hotspur
- **Teddy Sheringham** · Tottenham Hotspur

Player · Team*

Number of goals scored: 140, 160, 180, 200, 220, 240, 260

*The player spent most of his career with this team.

OWNING THE PICHICHI TROPHY

Like the English Premier League, La Liga in Spain features a collection of elite soccer stars. The player who leads the league in goals scored for the season wins the Pichichi Trophy. Lionel Messi and Cristiano Ronaldo have each won the Pichichi Trophy three times. Telmo Zarra won the scoring award six times—the most ever.

LIONEL MESSI

STATS FACT
A soccer ball can reach speeds of 100 miles (161 kilometers) per hour or more when it is kicked by a top player. The fastest recorded speed of a soccer ball after it was kicked is 131 miles (211 km) per hour by Ronny Heberson in 2006.

Most Goals Scored in a La Liga Season

PLAYER	TEAM	GOALS
Lionel Messi	Barcelona	50
Cristiano Ronaldo	Real Madrid	48
Lionel Messi	Barcelona	46
Cristiano Ronaldo	Real Madrid	46
Lionel Messi	Barcelona	43
Cristiano Ronaldo	Real Madrid	40
Hugo Sanchez	Real Madrid	38
Telmo Zarra	Athletic Bilbao	38
Baltazar	Atletico Madrid	35

THE ULTIMATE GOAL

Scoring a goal in any game is exciting. But scoring on the world's biggest soccer stage, with billions of people watching on TV and the Internet, means instant fame. Miroslav Klose did it five times during the 2002 World Cup. He scored five more times at the 2006 tournament, four times in 2010, and twice in 2014 when he led Germany to the World Cup crown. Klose retired in 2016 with 71 goals in international matches—the most in Germany's history—and his team never lost a game in which he scored.

Top Goal Scorers in World Cup History

Player · Country

- Miroslav Klose · Germany
- Ronaldo · Brazil
- Gerd Muller · West Germany
- Just Fontaine · France
- Pele · Brazil
- Jurgen Klinsmann · Germany
- Sandor Kocsis · Hungary
- Gabriel Batistuta · Argentina
- Teofilio Cubillas · Peru
- Grzegorz Lato · Poland
- Gary Lineker · England
- Thomas Muller · Germany
- Helmut Rahn · Germany

0 2 4 6 8 10 12 14 16

Total number of World Cup goals

MORE THAN A HAT TRICK

One player scoring three goals in a game is called a hat trick. It is a rare feat—unless you're a member of the United States Women's National Team (USWNT). Seven American women have scored five goals in a game—by far the most five-goal scorers of any nation.

ABBY WAMBACH

STATS FACT

The first hat trick scored in a World Cup was in 1930 by Bert Patenaude of the United States.

Most Goals in a Game by a USWNT Player

PLAYER	GOALS	SEASON	OPPONENT
Crystal Dunn	5	2016	Puerto Rico
Sydney Leroux	5	2012	Guatemala
Amy Rodriguez	5	2012	Dominican Republic
Abby Wambach	5	2004	Ireland
Tiffeny Milbrett	5	2002	Panama
Michelle Akers	5	1991	Chinese Taipei
Brandi Chastain	5	1991	Mexico

MAKING THE PLAY

The assist in soccer is a critical play that often doesn't get the respect it deserves from fans. Smart coaches put their best passers at the **midfielder** position, where they can move the ball to forwards for scoring chances. Of the top 10 all-time MLS assists leaders, only Jaime Moreno is not a midfielder.

HISTORY HIGHLIGHT

David Beckham might be the most successful player of his generation. Beckham starred in England for Manchester United and won six Premier League titles. In 2007 he won the La Liga crown with Real Madrid. Beckham joined MLS in 2007 and led the LA Galaxy to two championships.

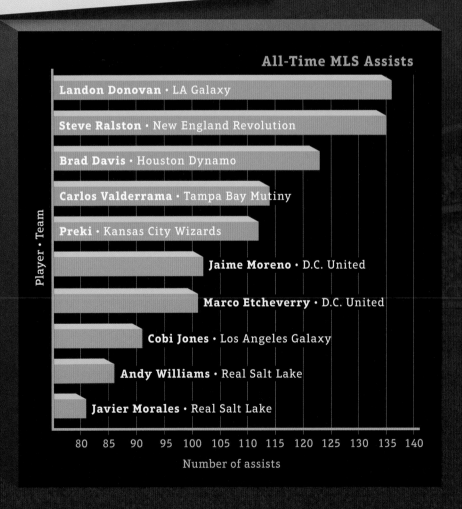

All-Time MLS Assists

Player • Team

- **Landon Donovan** · LA Galaxy
- **Steve Ralston** · New England Revolution
- **Brad Davis** · Houston Dynamo
- **Carlos Valderrama** · Tampa Bay Mutiny
- **Preki** · Kansas City Wizards
- **Jaime Moreno** · D.C. United
- **Marco Etcheverry** · D.C. United
- **Cobi Jones** · Los Angeles Galaxy
- **Andy Williams** · Real Salt Lake
- **Javier Morales** · Real Salt Lake

80 85 90 95 100 105 110 115 120 125 130 135 140

Number of assists

PASSING FANCY

Assists leaders are fine passers. But are they truly the best passers? What if a player makes great passes, but his teammates aren't so good at scoring?

Soccer leagues use advanced statistics to judge the skills of passers. Stats such as assists (AST), average passes per game (PPG), and percentage of passes completed successfully (P%) are all taken into account. Leagues use those numbers to give each passer a rating.

SEBASTIAN GIOVINCO

Top MLS Passers in 2016

PLAYER	TEAM	AST	PPG	P%	RATING
Sebastian Giovinco	Toronto FC	14	23.6	72.5	7.76
Osvaldo Alonso	Seattle Sounders	3	69.2	90.9	7.51
Sacha Kljestan	New York Red Bulls	16	49.8	74.8	7.42
David Villa	New York City FC	4	26.8	71.8	7.37
Ignacio Piatti	Montreal Impact	4	31.5	82.5	7.36
Walker Zimmerman	FC Dallas	0	42.4	78.4	7.30
Gyasi Zardes	LA Galaxy	5	27.5	71.1	7.29
Michael Bradley	Toronto FC	4	75.3	83.6	7.28
Bradley Wright-Phillips	New York Red Bulls	4	18.1	69.9	7.28
Mauro Diaz	FC Dallas	10	39.3	77.3	7.26

JOZY ALTIDORE

THAT'S THE POINT

Some players can score from anywhere on the field. Others have an incredible ability to know where their teammates are going to be and then hit them with pinpoint passes. The best players can do both.

Fans use points to keep track of a league's top players. A goal is worth two points. An assist is worth one point. Only one player can be credited with an assist on each goal.

US Men's National Team (USMNT) All-Time Points Leaders

PLAYER	GOALS	ASSISTS	POINTS
Landon Donovan	57	58	172
Clint Dempsey	48	13	109
Eric Wynalda	34	16	84
Brian McBride	30	10	70
Jozy Altidore	36	7	65
Joe-Max Moore	24	14	62
Cobi Jones	15	22	52
Bruce Murray	21	6	48

KEEPING A CLEAN SHEET

Soccer goalposts are 24 feet (7.3 meters) apart. The crossbar is 8 feet (2.4 m) high. That equals 192 square feet (18 sq. m) to defend. Preventing an attacking team from drilling the ball into the net takes quick reflexes and athleticism. The goalkeepers in MLS are among the world's elite athletes. They're all skilled at keeping the ball out of the net. The very best goalkeepers rack up a lot of **shutouts**, also called keeping a clean sheet.

Recent MLS Shutout Leaders

Year • Player • Team

- 2016 • **Luis Robles** • New York Red Bulls
- 2015 • **Adam Kwarasey** • Portland Timbers
- 2014 • **David Ousted** • Vancouver Whitecaps
- 2013 • **Donovan Ricketts** • Portland Timbers
- 2012 • **Jimmy Nielsen** • Sporting Kansas City
- 2011 • **Nick Rimando** • Real Salt Lake
- 2010 • **Nick Rimando** • Real Salt Lake
- 2009 • **Zach Thornton** • Chivas USA
- 2008 • **John Busch** • Chicago Fire
  - • **Kevin Hartman** • Kansas City Wizards
  - • **William Hesmer** • Columbus Crew
- 2007 • **Bradley Guzan** • Chivas USA

10   11   12   13   14   15

Number of shutouts

MEN OF THE MATCH

How do we rate the best overall performers on the **pitch**? In MLS, fans vote for a Man of the Match for each game. Fans choose the player who had the biggest impact on the game. That could be a key goal, a great pass, or a tough defensive play.

BRADLEY WRIGHT-PHILLIPS
(*TOP*)

Most MLS Man of the Match Awards in 2016		
PLAYER	**TEAM**	**AWARDS**
Sebastian Giovinco	Toronto FC	10
David Villa	New York City FC	9
Bradley Wright-Phillips	New York Red Bulls	9
Osvaldo Alonso	Seattle Sounders	6
David Accam	Chicago Fire	5
Fanendo Adi	Portland Timbers	5
Dominic Dwyer	Sporting Kansas City	5
Justin Meram	Columbus Crew	5

TIP OF THE CAP

In soccer's early years, FIFA didn't require that each player on a team wear the same jersey. Instead, they wore matching caps. When players joined their national teams, they received caps to wear. Players no longer receive hats. But the term *cap* still represents an appearance in an international match.

STATS FACT

From 1986 to 1990, the University of North Carolina women's soccer team went 103 straight games without losing. They won four national crowns during that stretch.

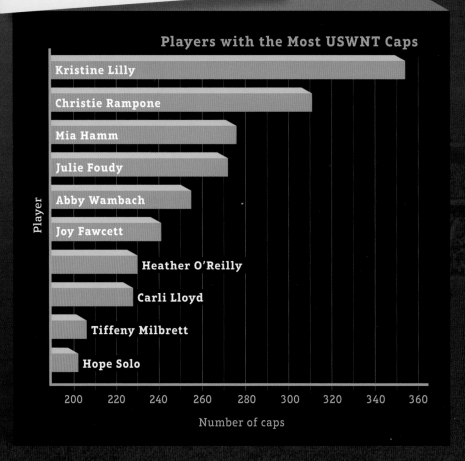

Players with the Most USWNT Caps

- Kristine Lilly
- Christie Rampone
- Mia Hamm
- Julie Foudy
- Abby Wambach
- Joy Fawcett
- Heather O'Reilly
- Carli Lloyd
- Tiffeny Milbrett
- Hope Solo

Player

Number of caps

200 220 240 260 280 300 320 340 360

CHAPTER TWO

TEAM SUPER STATS

RAISING THE CUP

The World Cup trophy weighs about 13 pounds (5.9 kilograms) and is covered in gold. As many as 200 national teams compete in qualifying matches to reach the World Cup tournament. The tournament lasts one month, with 32 teams competing for the trophy. Eight nations have won the World Cup since the first tournament in 1930.

GERMANY IN 2014

Men's World Cup Champions

TEAM	WINS	YEARS WON
Brazil	5	1958, 1962, 1970, 1994, 2002
Italy	4	1934, 1938, 1982, 2006
West Germany	3	1954, 1974, 1990
Argentina	2	1978, 1986
Uruguay	2	1930, 1950
Germany	1	2014
Spain	1	2010
France	1	1998
England	1	1966

STATS FACT
Brazil is the only country to qualify for all 19 World Cup tournaments.

NEYMAR

STRIKING GOLD!

When Neymar scored the winning **penalty kick** to win the gold medal at the 2016 Olympic Games, it gave host nation Brazil its first Olympic gold medal in soccer. Brazil became the 19th country to win the men's gold since soccer became an Olympic sport in 1900. The closest the United States has come is second place in 1904. Five countries have struck gold more than once.

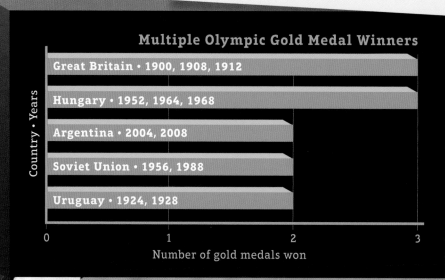

Multiple Olympic Gold Medal Winners

Great Britain • 1900, 1908, 1912

Hungary • 1952, 1964, 1968

Argentina • 2004, 2008

Soviet Union • 1956, 1988

Uruguay • 1924, 1928

Country • Years

Number of gold medals won

0   1   2   3

US WOMEN LEAD THE WORLD

Since the USWNT was formed in 1985, it has dominated women's soccer around the world. The United States has won more international matches, scored more goals, had longer winning streaks, and collected more gold medals than any other team in international women's soccer history.

STATS FACT

The USWNT won the first Women's World Cup in 1991 by defeating Norway, 2–1. The US team had beaten its previous five opponents by a combined score of 49–0.

2015 USWNT

Women's World Cup Champions

COUNTRY	WORLD CUP CROWNS	YEARS
United States	3	1991, 1999, 2015
Germany	2	2003, 2007
Japan	1	2011
Norway	1	1995

Women's Olympic Champions

COUNTRY	OLYMPIC GOLD MEDALS	YEARS
United States	4	1996, 2004, 2008, 2012
Germany	1	2016
Norway	1	2000

YOU CAN'T SCORE IF YOU DON'T SHOOT

The number of shots per game (SPG) a team takes is an important stat for understanding how well they played on offense. But many of those shots may miss their target. An even more important number is shots on goal per game (SGPG). This stat tells fans how many shots would have been goals if the other team hadn't stopped them.

MANCHESTER CITY *(LEFT)*
VS. PARIS SAINT-GERMAIN

HISTORY HIGHLIGHT

Many fans consider Pele the greatest soccer player of all time. He grew up in Brazil in extreme poverty and developed his soccer skills by kicking a sock stuffed with rags. He led Brazil to three World Cup titles—the only player ever to win the world's top soccer prize three times—and finished his career with 1,281 goals, the most ever.

Top Shooting Teams in Europe in 2016

TEAM	LEAGUE	SPG	SGPG
Tottenham Hotspur	Premier League	18.7	6.5
Barcelona	La Liga	16.4	6
Borussia Dortmund	Bundesliga	14.1	5.8
Lyon	Ligue 1	14.9	5.8
Manchester City	Premier League	16.9	5.8
Chelsea	Premier League	15.4	5.6
Atletico Madrid	La Liga	14.4	5.2
Arsenal	Premier League	14.3	4.7
Marseilles	Ligue 1	11.4	4.1
Lille	Ligue 1	12.6	3.9

CREATING WAYS TO SCORE

Soccer teams score in different ways. Most goals are scored in open play (OP), the normal flow of a soccer match. Some teams are better at scoring on a counterattack (CA)—taking the ball on defense and streaking to the other end for a quick goal. Other teams are dangerous during a **set piece** (SP) after play has been stopped by the referee. Or a team might have a great shooter who can score on a penalty kick (PK).

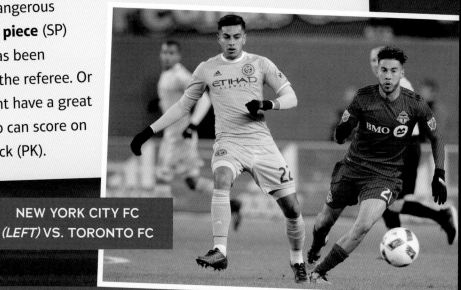

NEW YORK CITY FC
(LEFT) VS. TORONTO FC

How the MLS Playoff Teams Scored in 2016

TEAM	OP	CA	SP	PK
Colorado Rapids	29	0	8	2
D.C. United	36	3	11	3
FC Dallas	31	3	10	5
LA Galaxy	38	3	7	4
Montreal Impact	30	3	11	5
New York City FC	42	5	9	6
New York Red Bulls	37	1	20	1
Philadelphia Union	32	1	11	6
Real Salt Lake	26	1	9	6
Seattle Sounders	29	1	10	3
Sporting Kansas City	24	0	13	5
Toronto FC	33	3	11	4

DE-FENSE! DE-FENSE!

Comparing teams by their scoring is easy. But how can we rate soccer teams defensively? The most important stat is goals conceded, the number of goals scored against a team. It tells the story of how a team's entire defense comes together to stop opponents from scoring.

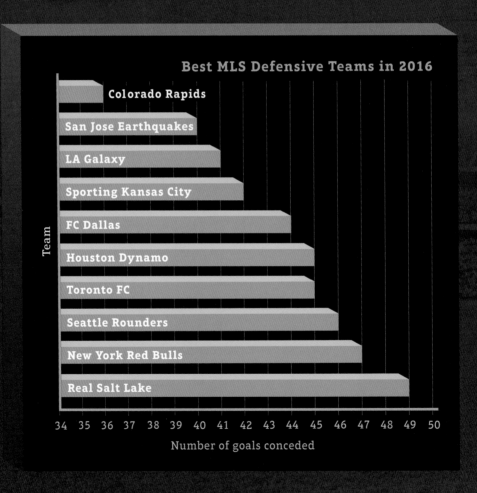

Best MLS Defensive Teams in 2016

Team

- Colorado Rapids
- San Jose Earthquakes
- LA Galaxy
- Sporting Kansas City
- FC Dallas
- Houston Dynamo
- Toronto FC
- Seattle Rounders
- New York Red Bulls
- Real Salt Lake

34 35 36 37 38 39 40 41 42 43 44 45 46 47 48 49 50

Number of goals conceded

FIERCE DEFENSE

Teams work hard to prevent the other team from scoring—sometimes a little too hard. A strong **tackle** can stop a goal-scoring chance before it starts. Of course, rough play often leads to **fouls** if players aren't careful. The best defenses walk a thin line between fierce tackling and getting too many fouls.

2016 NEW YORK RED BULLS

How the MLS Playoff Teams Played Defense in 2016

TEAM	TACKLES PER GAME	FOULS PER GAME
Colorado Rapids	16.9	13.5
DC United	19.6	14.9
FC Dallas	18.7	13
LA Galaxy	16.2	10.6
Montreal Impact	17.8	12.7
New York City FC	20.9	12.3
New York Red Bulls	21.3	13.2
Philadelphia Union	18.7	11.4
Real Salt Lake	16.9	12.8
Seattle Sounders	15.9	10.3
Sporting Kansas City	19.1	12.4
Toronto FC	18.1	10.6

CHAPTER THREE

STATS ARE HERE TO STAY

THE BOX SCORE

The rules of soccer have changed over time, but fans have always looked to stats to tell the stories of the sport. A contest in England between teams from Sheffield and London in 1866 was the first official game to last 90 minutes. (Modern matches still last 90 minutes.) Statistics from the match were recorded in a box score. The numbers told who scored goals and when they were scored—the story of the match.

A box score today contains much more information than was recorded in 1866. Take a look at the box score on the next page to see an account of the 2015 Women's World Cup championship match between the United States and Japan. It has all the stats a fan wants to know about a soccer match. What do all these words and numbers mean? Use the key below to read the box score.

Key
SA = shots attempted
SOG = shots on goal
MS = missed shots
BS = blocked shots
FC = fouls committed
C = corner kicks
FK = free kicks
S = saves

CARLI LLOYD
(LEFT)

2015 WORLD CUP CHAMPIONSHIP MATCH
United States 5, Japan 2

SCORING SUMMARY

USA	Carli Lloyd	3rd minute (of the match)
USA	Carli Lloyd	5th minute
USA	Lauren Holiday	14th minute
USA	Carli Lloyd	16th minute
JPN	Yuki Ogimi	27th minute
JPN	Julie Johnston (own goal)	52nd minute
USA	Tobin Heath	54th minute

UNITED STATES	
SA	15
SOG	7
MS	4
BS	4
FC	14
C	7
FK	11
S	3

JAPAN	
SA	12
SOG	4
MS	4
BS	4
FC	10
C	3
FK	15
S	2

STAT STRATEGY

For both players and fans, stats have never been more important. Fans love to follow the stats of their favorite teams and players around the world. Players use stats to plan for opponents. For example, defenders know if a player is likely to pass or shoot based on his stats, and they use that information to try to stop him.

Coaches use statistics to design game plans. Perhaps a team's next opponent often scores on the counterattack. Then the coach may order his defenders to stay closer than usual to their own goal.

FANTASY AND THE FUTURE

Fantasy soccer is wildly popular in Europe, and it is catching on in the United States and Canada. It's a contest that adult fans play using the stats of real players. To play, fans choose players from leagues such as MLS to form fantasy teams. Most fantasy games are played online.

Websites and television networks around the world analyze soccer stats and provide advice for fantasy players. One study showed that 56.8 million people in the United States and Canada played fantasy sports in 2015. The number of people playing fantasy soccer is growing!

STATS MATCHUP

Most soccer fans around the world agree that Lionel Messi and Cristiano Ronaldo are the two best soccer players in the sport. Messi plays in La Liga for FC Barcelona. He's also the star player on Argentina's national team. When he races around the pitch, fans call it Messi magic.

Lionel Messi

Career matches played	671
Career goals	537
Career assists	222
International games played	116
International goals	57
International assists	37

LIONEL MESSI

Ronaldo plays for the Spanish club Real Madrid and Portugal's national team. He's a huge celebrity. He's also the world's best-paid athlete— one spot ahead of Messi. Both players can score from anywhere on the pitch. But who is better? You decide.

Cristiano Ronaldo

Career matches played	829
Career goals	537
Career assists	189
International games played	136
International goals	68
International assists	23

CRISTIANO RONALDO

GLOSSARY

corner kick: a free kick from a corner of the field near the goal after the ball goes out of bounds across the end line

foul: an action by a player that referees think is unfair or against the rules

free kick: a kick made without being defended by the other team, awarded by the referee after a foul

midfielder: a player who usually stays in the middle of the field and is responsible for both offense and defense

penalty kick: a free kick at the goal from about 12 yards away, awarded by the referee after a foul near the goal

pitch: a soccer field

set piece: a play that takes place after the game has been stopped. A set piece is usually a free kick, a corner kick, or a throw-in.

shutout: a game in which the losing team doesn't score

tackle: a defensive play that stops a player with the ball from advancing with it

FURTHER INFORMATION

Crisfield, Deborah. *The Everything Kids' Soccer Book*. Avon, MA: Adams Media, 2015.

Fishman, Jon M. *Lionel Messi*. Minneapolis: Lerner Publications, 2018.

Mills, Andrea. *The Soccer Book: Facts and Terrific Trivia*. Buffalo: Firefly Books, 2016.

Major League Soccer
http://www.mlssoccer.com

US Soccer
http://www.ussoccer.com

US Youth Soccer
http://www.usyouthsoccer.org

INDEX

PHOTO ACKNOWLEDGMENTS

The images in this book are used with the permission of: © Laura Westlund/Independent Picture Service (charts); © iStockphoto.com/sArhange1, p. 1 (backgrounds); © iStockphoto.com/Pali Rao, p. 1; © Victor Decolongon/Getty Images, p. 4; © Bob Thomas/Popperfoto/Getty Images, p. 5; © Photo by Tim Clayton/Corbis/Getty Images, p. 6; © David Ramos/Getty Images, p. 8; © Chris Graythen/Getty Images, p. 10; © Kevin Sousa/Icon SMI, p. 12; © Frederick Breedon/Getty Images, p. 13; © Jeff Zelevansk/Getty Images, p. 15; © Sampics/Sampics/Corbis/Getty Images, p. 17; © Stuart Franklin/FIFA/Getty Images, p. 18; © Dennis Grombkowski/Getty Images, p. 19; © Alex Livesey/Getty Images, p. 20; © Tim Clayton/Corbis/Getty Images, pp. 21, 23; © FIFA/Getty Images, p. 25; © GENIA SAVILOV/AFP/Getty Images, p. 26; © svetikd/E+/Getty Images, p. 27; © VI Images/Getty Images, p. 28; © Matt Roberts/Getty Images, p. 29.

Front cover: © iStockphoto.com/Pali Rao.